Some of
the World's
Weirdest and
Wackiest Animals

David R Morgan

illustrated by Ferro Sandityo

A2Z
PRESS

Some of the World's Weirdest and Wackiest Animals

This is a work of fiction.

Printed in the United States of America

A 2 Z Press LLC

PO Box 582

Deleon Springs, FL 32130

bestlittleonlinebookstorecom

sizemore3630@aol.com

440-241-3126

ISBN: 978-1-946908-43-8

Dedication

To Bex and Toby,
Who are my
Wonders in this world!

Some of the world's
weirdest & wackiest animals

are in this book...

WEIRD
ANIMALS

So let's turn a few pages
and have a good look...

...at the **Shoebill, Sea Pig, Panda Ant,**
the **Giant Isopod,** The **Goblin Shark** and more

...all amazing and quite odd!

The Hairy Panda Ants are wasps and
their females have no wings,

They are Found in Chile, sipping nectar,
and buzzing as they sing.

Yes, they look just like an ant dressed up like a panda,
but let me tell you now..

These cute critter's **little sting** can stun a great big cow!

The Giant Isopod can be seen scuttling
in the ocean's dark and deep,

they look like a **supergiant** pill bug
that also rolls as they creep,

It is a crustacean related
to the **shrimp** and **crab**,

Isopods have eyes that glow
and they have claws that grab.

Over there's the **Pangolin**,
a termite loving creature,
you can tell....

RUN!!

KERATIN

For 80 million years it has kept safe by its **keratin shell.**

Keratin? That is fingernails to you and me,

The Pangolin
is perfect but is an
**endangered
species.**

The Axolotl (ak•suh•laa•tl) is the Mexican walking 'fish,'

It can repair itself and belongs in its own niche.

It is a small salamander...
an amphibian, you see,

Who can grow back
any part of its own body.

The little **Hummingbird Hawk-Moth** feeds on flowers,

And like the Hummingbird, it flashes lovely colors.

From Greece to Japan,
the **Hummingbird Hawk-Moth** looks great,

This insect was discovered
by Carl Linnaeus in 1758.

There is a Red-Lipped Bat-Fish
who cannot swim so well,

They sit on the ocean floor
by the **Galapagos Island**, please do tell.

How the Red-Lipped Bat-Fish uses
adapted pectoral fins to take a slow walk,

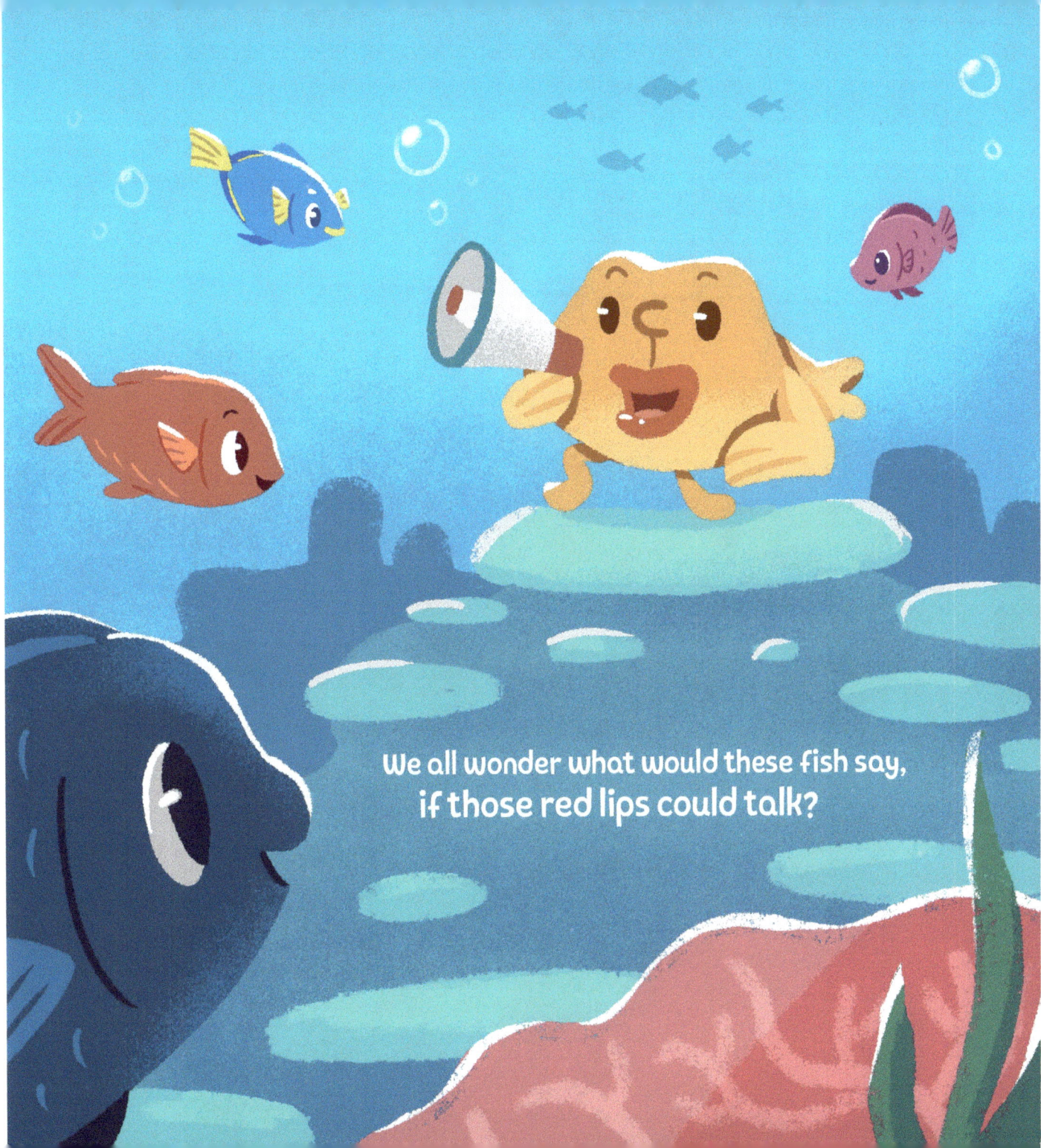

We all wonder what would these fish say,
if those red lips could talk?

AND here's the **Shoebill**, a large stork-like bird,

With a **beak like a shoe** and the strangest call, so I've ever heard.

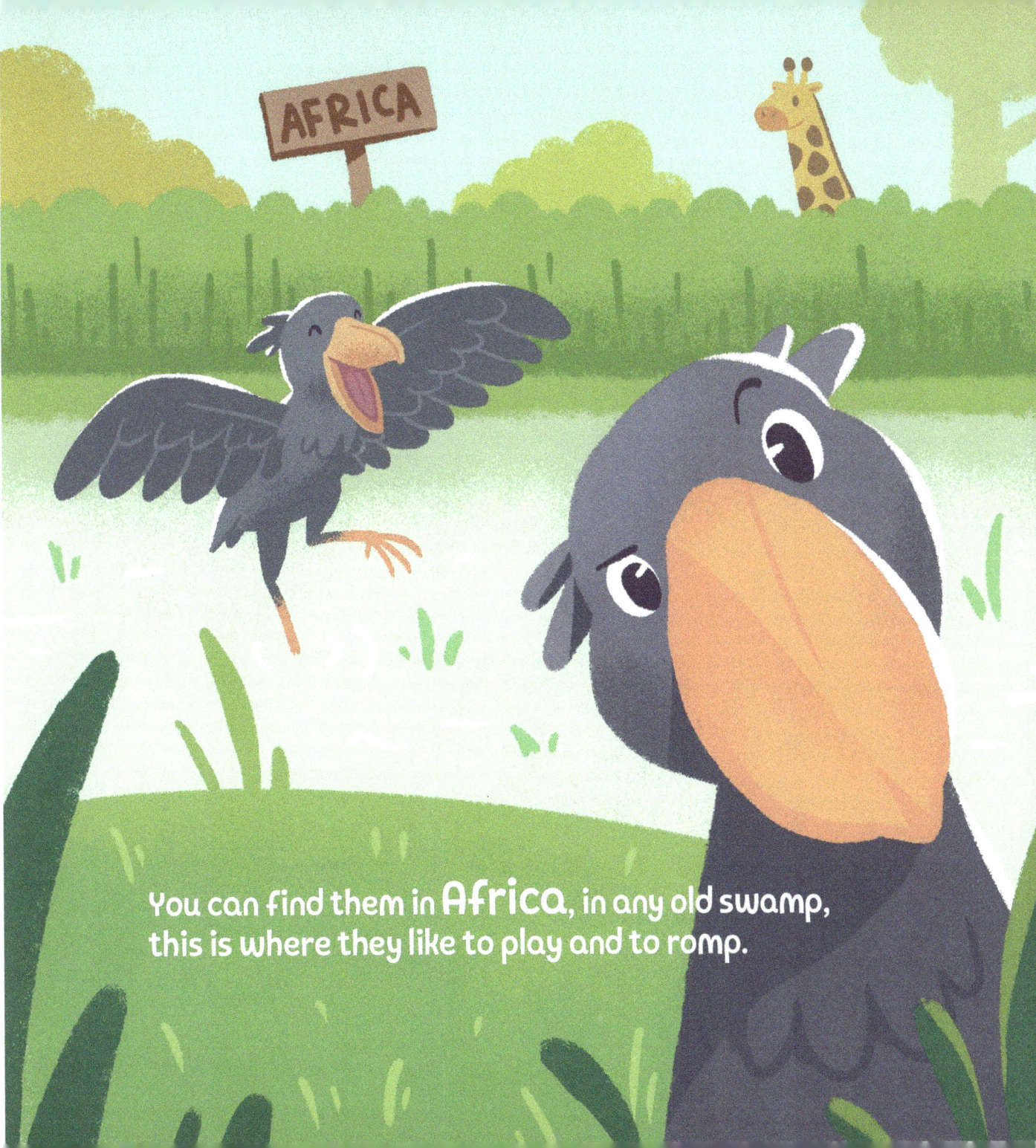

You can find them in **Africa**, in any old swamp, this is where they like to play and to romp.

The Russian **Saiga Antelope** has a large and flexible nose,

That filters dust and helps keep their body temperature low, so their story goes.

They can live 12 years in the wild and you will find,
They have amazing eyesight and are very kind.

Hello **Narwhal** – known as the unicorn of the sea,
Narwhals live in the cold waters of the Artic I do decree!

They have a saber-like tooth that can grow to 10 feet long,

10ft.

And talk to each other with high pitched clicks,
whistles, squeaks and bangs
– their magical song.

Oh look, the little **Sea Pig**'s found 4000 feet below,
In the cold ocean, on seven pairs of feet, they go.

4000ft

With a little hook-like nose, this truffle-hunting pig,
Is a pink-bodied creature who surely likes to dig.

And we must let's not forget ...

　　　..the **Long-Horned Weaver Spider** that roams,

The forests and fields of **Asia** — but PLEASE not in our homes!

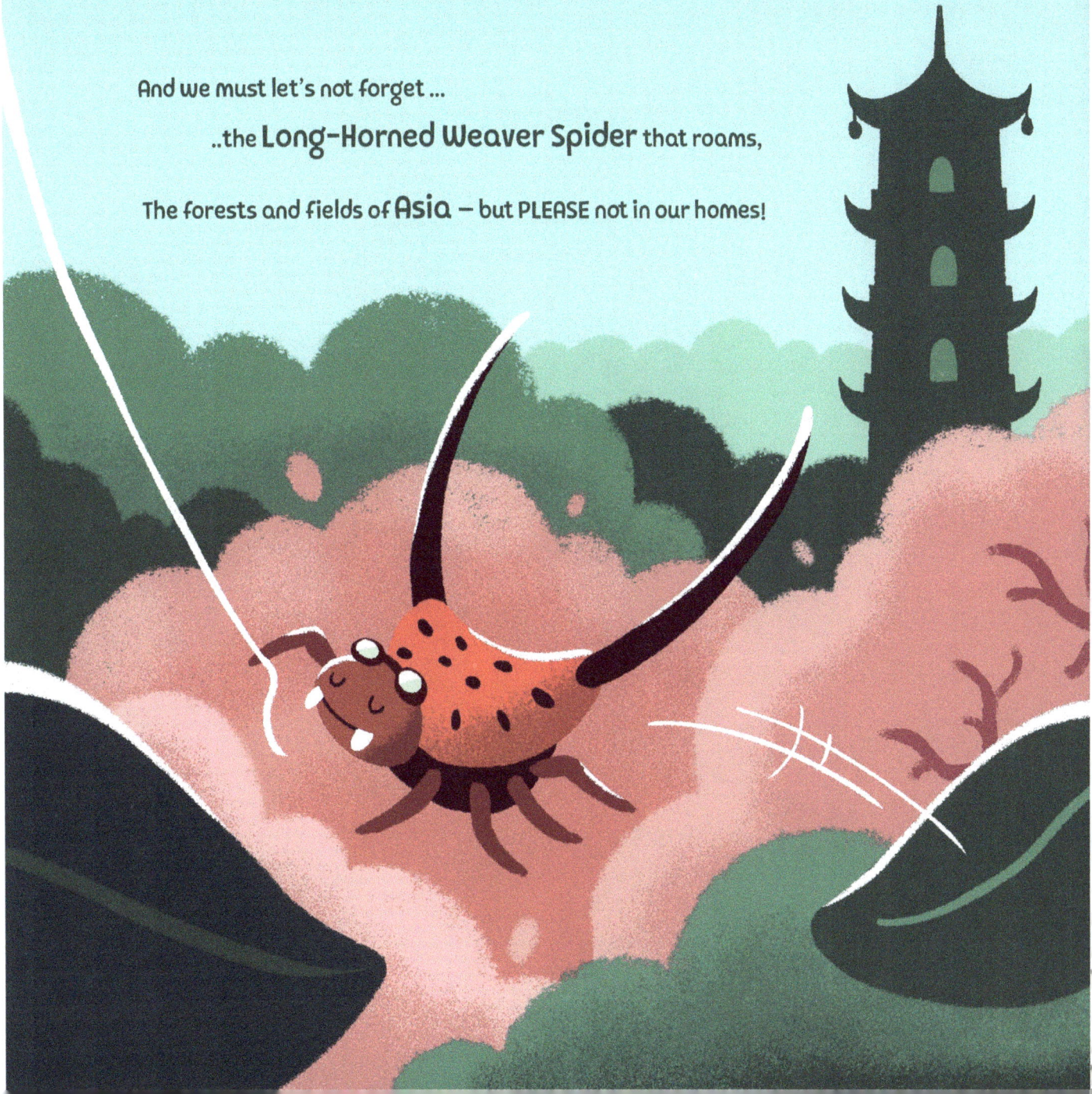

With **two long horns** that look like tools for WIFI,
This pretty spider and its web are a feast for the eye.

The **Gharial** is a skinny snouted croc
in **India**'s waterways,

They have 110 teeth, but there are
only 235 are Gharials left these days.

They are large and heavy with weak legs, so near Delhi,
You can see this reptile simply sliding on its belly!

Golly! The Goblin Shark looks like a living fossil,
He can grow to 14 feet, which is truly colossal!

Very little is known
about this bubble pink shark,

With its strange-looking
broad snout that is very stark.

Whether they are in the **sky**, on **land**, or in the **sea**,
These are some of the weirdest creatures you will ever see.

They have odd bodies, strange habits, or a funny face,
But all these creatures do make this world an interesting place.

The End

Meet the....

Shoe billed stork also known as the whale-headed stork,

and the Giant Isopod found in cold, deep sea waters,

and the Panda Ant discovered in 1938 and lives in Chili.

And meet the....

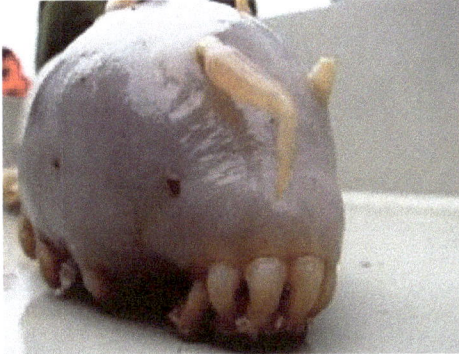

The Sea pig that lives in the deepest part of the ocean,

and the cute Pangolin that is endangered! Please save,

and the freaky scary Pink Goblin Shark considered to be a living fossil.

And also meet the....

Axolotl - the Mexican walking fish, is really an amphibian,

and the Long-Horned Weaver Spider found in Asian and India,

and the Red-Lipped Batfish with its bright red lips!

And also meet the....

The Russian Saiga Antelope with its beautiful nose!

and the Narwhal— the whale known as the unicorn of the sea!

and the humming-bird hawk-moth that can be found from Portugal to Japan.

And lastly, meet the....

Gharial that is among the longest living of all croco-diles! And has many sharp teeth!

We know there are many, many more! Have fun finding them!

David R Morgan lives in England. He is a talented full-time teacher and writer.

He has written music, journalism, poetry, and children's books. His books for children include: 'The Strange Case of William Whipper-Snapper,' three 'Info Rider' books for Collins and 'Blooming Cats' which won the Acorn Award and was animated for television. He has also written a Horrible Histories biography: ' Spilling The Beans On Boudicca' and stories for Children's anthologies.

For the last four years he has been working on his Soundings Project with his son Toby, performing his own poetry/writing to Toby's original music. This work is on   YouTube, Spotify, and Soundcloud.

Other Books by David R. Morgan

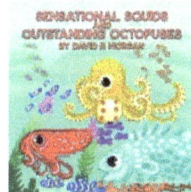

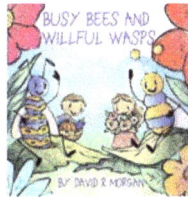

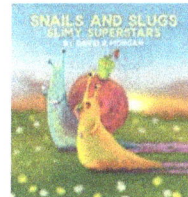

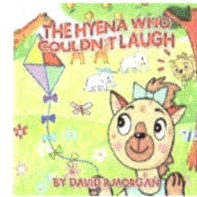

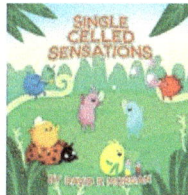

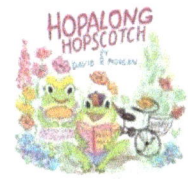

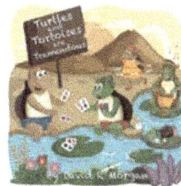

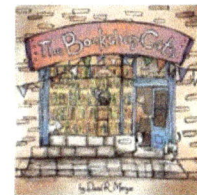

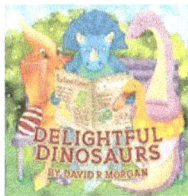

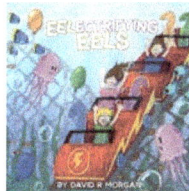

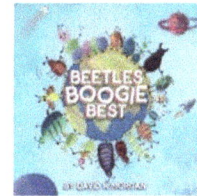

Ants are fANTastic

SENSATIONAL SQUIDS AND OUTSTANDING OCTOPUSES
BY DAVID R MORGAN

BUSY BEES AND WILLFUL WASPS
BY DAVID R MORGAN

SNAILS AND SLUGS SLIMY SUPERSTARS
BY DAVID R MORGAN

THE HYENA WHO COULDN'T LAUGH
BY DAVID R MORGAN

AWE INSPIRING OWLS
BY DAVID R MORGAN

Wonderful Wriggling Whirling Worms
by David R Morgan

SINGLE CELLED SENSATIONS
BY DAVID R MORGAN

HOPALONG HOPSCOTCH
BY DAVID R MORGAN

Butterfly Beauties and Magical Moths
by David R Morgan

STUNNING SNAKES ARE HAPPY HISSERS
BY DAVID R MORGAN

Turtles and Tortoises Tremendous!

COOL COWS AND BLAZING BULLS
BY DAVID R MORGAN

FABULOUS FROGS AND TERRIFIC TOADS

The Bookshop Cat

DELIGHTFUL DINOSAURS
BY DAVID R MORGAN

ELECTRIFYING EELS
BY DAVID R MORGAN

RUNAWAY RAGTIME

CRABS ARE INCRABABLE

BEETLES BOOGIE BEST

And many more to come!

www.ingramcontent.com/pod-product-compliance
Lightning Source LLC
Chambersburg PA
CBHW051312020426
42333CB00027B/3304